Withdrawn

Superstar Cars

Lamborghini

James Bow

CRABTREE
Publishing Company
www.crabtreebooks.com

Superstar Cars

Author: James Bow
Publishing plan research and development:
  Sean Charlebois, Reagan Miller
  Crabtree Publishing Company
Editor: Sonya Newland
Proofreader: Molly Aloian
Editorial director: Kathy Middleton
Project coordinator and prepress technician: Margaret Salter
Print coordinator: Katherine Berti
Series consultant: Petrina Gentile
Cover design: Ken Wright
Design: Paul Cherrill
Photo research: Amy Sparks

Photographs:
Alamy: Colin Curwood: p. 11; imagebroker: p. 17;
  Oleksiy Maksymenko: p. 24, 30–31; Phil Talbot: p. 37, 49;
  culture-images GmbH: p. 39; Alvey & Towers Picture
  Library: p. 42; Jonathan Tennant: p. 48
Corbis: Transtock: p. 8; Rick Maiman/Sygma: p. 38; Car
  Culture: p. 45
Dreamstime: Disegnos: p. 34–35
Lamborghini: p. 1, 6–7, 9, 12, 13, 14, 16, 21, 22–23, 23, 24–25,
  26, 26–27, 29, 31, 32, 35, 40, 41, 43, 46, 47, 50, 51, 52, 53, 54,
  55, 56, 56–57, 58–59, 59
Motoring Picture Library: p. 18–19, 20, 33, 36, 44;
  Tom Wood: p. 5, 10, 15
Shutterstock: front cover; Christoff: p. 4

Library and Archives Canada Cataloguing in Publication

Bow, James, 1972-
    Lamborghini / James Bow.

(Superstar cars)
Includes index.
Issued also in an electronic format.
ISBN 978-0-7787-2144-4 (bound).--ISBN 978-0-7787-2151-2 (pbk.)

    1. Lamborghini automobile--Juvenile literature.
I. Title. II. Series: Superstar cars

TL215.L33B69 2011   j629.222'2   C2010-905632-9

Library of Congress Cataloging-in-Publication Data

Bow, James.
 Lamborghini / James Bow.
    p. cm. -- (Superstar cars)
Includes index.
ISBN 978-0-7787-2151-2 (pbk. : alk. paper) --
ISBN 978-0-7787-2144-4 (reinforced library binding : alk. paper) --
ISBN 978-1-4271-9549-4 (electronic (pdf))
 1. Lamborghini automobile--Juvenile literature. I. Title. II. Series.

TL215.L33B69 2010
629.222'2--dc22

                                              2010034936

Crabtree Publishing Company

www.crabtreebooks.com   1-800-387-7650

Printed in the U.S.A./102010/SP20100915

Published in Canada
Crabtree Publishing
616 Welland Ave.
St. Catharines, ON
L2M 5V6

Published in the United States
Crabtree Publishing
PMB 59051
350 Fifth Avenue, 59th Floor
New York, New York 10118

Published in the United Kingdom
Crabtree Publishing
Maritime House
Basin Road North, Hove
BN41 1WR

Published in Australia
Crabtree Publishing
386 Mt. Alexander Rd.
Ascot Vale (Melbourne)
VIC 3032

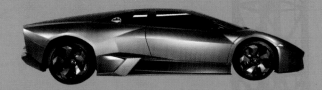

>> Contents

1 From Tractors to Cars   4

2 The First Lamborghini   10

3 Lamborghini Rises   18

4 Lamborghini After Ferruccio   28

5 Chrysler Joins In   38

6 Stability, Growth, Acclaim   46

7 Driving Into the Future   56

Lamborghini Timeline   60

Further Information   61

Glossary   62

Index   64

Chapter 1

From Tractors to Cars »»»»

Lamborghinis are not your average car. They're not even your average luxury car. They are some of the most expensive cars on the planet. They are powerful cars, driven by 12-cylinder engines capable of 670 **horsepower**—as much power as your average 18-wheeler truck. In expert hands, they can hit 211 mph (340 km/h) and can go from 0 to 60 mph (97 km/h) in 2.8 seconds.

The car of choice

Lamborghinis do not have fully **automatic transmissions** and not all have stability control systems. They are not cars that take care of drivers. They are cars that drivers control. That is what their drivers want—to have control over unmatched power in a car that has been designed with elegance. They may be driven by princes and billionaires, but believe it or not, Lamborghinis were invented by a tractor maker.

Everything in a Lamborghini's design and construction epitomizes supercar style and power.

Ferruccio Lamborghini

When Lamborghini was founded in 1963, Italy was home to famous car companies like Fiat, Ferrari, Maserati, and Alfa Romeo. It was a crowded field, but within two years, Lamborghini had taken its place alongside these companies as a maker of great fast and fancy cars.

It had an unlikely beginning. Ferruccio Lamborghini, the company's founder, was born on a grape farm in 1916. As a young man he preferred fixing equipment to tending grapes. Seeing his talent, his parents sent him to a technical institute near Bologna to study mechanics. In 1940, he was drafted into the Royal Italian Air Force, where he served as a mechanic during World War II.

Returning home after the war, Ferruccio opened an auto repair shop and garage.

Italy needs tractors

Times were hard in postwar Italy. Farmers in particular had a problem— there were no tractors. The country's auto plants had been building war equipment since the late 1930s. What tractors could be found were old and run down. To solve this problem, Ferruccio Lamborghini took parts from abandoned military equipment and built a tractor for his parents. People were so impressed by the Lamborghini family's new tractor that neighbors asked Ferruccio to build tractors for them, as well.

The charging bull logo is now recognized all over the world as the badge of a car in a class of its own.

The charging bull

Ferruccio Lamborghini was fascinated by bullfighting. In 1962, just before founding Automobili Lamborghini, he visited the ranch of Don Eduardo Miura, a famous breeder of Spanish fighting bulls. Ferruccio was so impressed by the animals that he adopted the image of the raging bull as the emblem for his company. Several of his car models have bullfighting-related names, including the Murciélago, the Urraco, the Jalpa, and the Miura.

5

Lamborghini Tractori

By 1948, Ferruccio had established Lamborghini Tractori, which he operated out of his garage. Within two years, the company produced over 1,000 tractors. By 1960, Lamborghini Tractori was one of Italy's largest manufacturers of agricultural equipment—and Ferruccio was one of the richest men in the country.

Not fast enough?

Ferruccio Lamborghini loved fast cars. He had enough Alfa Romeos and Maseratis to drive a different one every day of the week. The cars were the best on the market, but none of them pleased him. "They felt heavy and did not really go very fast," he said. Ferruccio wanted a **grand tourer**—or "gran turismo," in Italian—a vehicle to speed the driver across the countryside in luxury, with controls that responded quickly to the driver's command.

In search of perfection

In an interview with *Sporting Motorist* magazine in 1964, Ferruccio said, "I have bought some of the most expensive gran turismo cars and in each of these magnificent cars I have found some faults. Too hot. Or uncomfortable. Or not sufficiently fast. Or not perfectly finished. Now I want to make a GT car without faults." Ferruccio bought a Ferrari 250 GT in 1958. Putting the car through its paces, he would often grind the gears, forcing him to take the car back to Ferrari to be fixed.

Lamborghini's founder, Ferruccio, with one of his supercars—and one of his famous tractors!

On water

Although Lamborghini saw himself
as a car builder, in 1968 he couldn't
resist installing a four-liter V12 engine on
a powerboat. Lamborghini prototyped a boat
called the "Quetzal" but decided instead
to supply the engines for offshore racing.
In 1984, Count Renato della Valle used
a Lamborghini engine to win the round-
Britain race. More recently, an 8.2-liter
V12 Lamborghini engine powered
the boat "Spirit of Norway"
to victory in 2002.

7

Modified Ferraris

Enzo Ferrari was secretive about the manufacture of his cars. Garage mechanics would take cars to the back and not let their owners watch the work being done—something that angered mechanic Ferruccio. He took matters into his own hands, modifying his Ferrari 250 GT with parts from his tractors. When he found that his modified car could outperform Ferrari's stock models, he took his concerns to Enzo Ferrari himself.

Lamborghini vs. Ferrari

To hear Ferruccio tell it, the first meeting between Lamborghini and Ferrari did not go well. "I had to wait for him a very long time," he explained. "'Ferrari, your cars are rubbish!' I complained. Il Commendatore was furious. 'Lamborghini, you may be able to drive a tractor but you will never be able to handle a Ferrari properly.'" According to Lamborghini, this was the moment he decided to make a perfect car.

The rivalry between Ferrari (red) and Lamborghini (yellow) started in the 1960s. Even today, supercar fans are often loyal to one make or the other.

The Lamborghini legend

Did it really happen that way? Skeptics point out that Lamborghini knew he could make more money building his own cars than helping Ferrari improve his. But the confrontation between Lamborghini and Ferrari is part of the Lamborghini legend. Whatever the case, by 1963, Ferruccio was committed to entering the auto-making business. But he also knew that he was challenging the giants of the Italian auto industry. To stand out among such names as Ferrari, Maserati, and Fiat, his car would have to be perfect.

A crowded field

Several carmakers were already well established by the time Ferruccio set up Lamborghini. These formed the competition. Some of the main companies were:
Alfa Romeo: established 1910
Casalini: established 1939
Ferrari: established 1929
Fiat: established 1899
Lancia: established 1906
Maserati: established 1914

By 1963, Ferruccio Lamborghini was ready to step up to the challenge of creating a better car than his rival, Ferrari.

Chapter 2
The First Lamborghini »»»»

Lamborghini, the automotive company, began in 1963, when Ferruccio established Automobili Lamborghini. He was a skilled mechanic and a man of vision—and he wanted to build the perfect car—but he was also a savvy businessman. He knew he couldn't build his dream car and sell it to the world all on his own. Before he could bend metal or shape glass, his first task was establishing a team of some of the best and brightest engineers and mechanics to design and build his vehicle.

The Lamborghini team

In building his perfect car, Ferruccio started with the engine. For this, he contacted Giotto Bizzarrini, Ferrari's former chief engineer. Bizzarrini had left Ferrari in 1961 during a personal dispute with owner Enzo Ferrari and had worked since then building racecar engines. Bizzarrini designed and built Lamborghini's engine in four months. It was a V12, 3.4-liter engine with twin overhead **camshafts**, all built from aluminum **alloy**.

The first Lamborghini-designed engine was powerful and light. Its reduced weight increased speed.

Engineering genius

Then Lamborghini brought aboard Giampaolo Dallara to act as chief engineer. Dallara had worked for Ferrari and Maserati in their design departments. His first task for Lamborghini was to design a **chassis** to support the powerful engine. Dallara went on to help design the 350 GT, the Miura, the Islero, and the Espada. Dallara brought aboard recent college graduate Giampaolo Stanzani and a New Zealand racecar driver named Bob Wallace as part of Lamborghini's original engineering team.

Bring in the designers...

Finally, freelance designer Franco Scaglione was brought in to design a body to rest atop the chassis. Franco had already been responsible for dozens of designs for such carmakers as Fiat, Alfa Romeo, Maserati, and Porsche.

Giampaolo Dallara

Giampaolo Dallara was born in 1936 and studied engineering. He was recruited by Ferrari in 1959. Although he worked only a short while at Ferrari before moving to Maserati, he impressed Giotto Bizzarrini, Ferrari's chief engineer, enough that when Lamborghini talked to Bizzarrini about the 350 GTV, he suggested Dallara as Lamborghini's chief engineer. He left Lamborghini in 1969 to design Formula 1 racecars.

Today, Giampaolo Dallara is still designing and building cars, including Formula 1 chassis, this time for a team called Campos Grand Prix.

11

A place to build

With the team together, they needed a place to work. Ferruccio set aside a corner of his tractor factory for work on the **prototype**, while work began on a new factory in the town of Sant'Agata, between Modena and Bologna. It wasn't far from where his competitors were working, but it wasn't far from the companies that supplied his competitors with parts, either. The area had the suppliers Ferruccio needed to make his dream car a reality.

A big investment

Ferruccio built his factory on a "**greenfield**" site outside of town, where land was cheap, leaving himself plenty of room for expansion. In total, Ferruccio invested around US$305,000 of his own fortune to launch his company. This is equivalent to more than US$2 million today.

Launch of the Lamborghini

The small Lamborghini team scrambled and, in just four months they debuted their first car—the Lamborghini 350 GTV—at the Turin Auto Show in October 1963. It certainly turned heads. Scaglione's design produced a beautiful automobile with a low hood and an extra-large rear window. It was lower, sleeker, and faster-looking than anything else on the road.

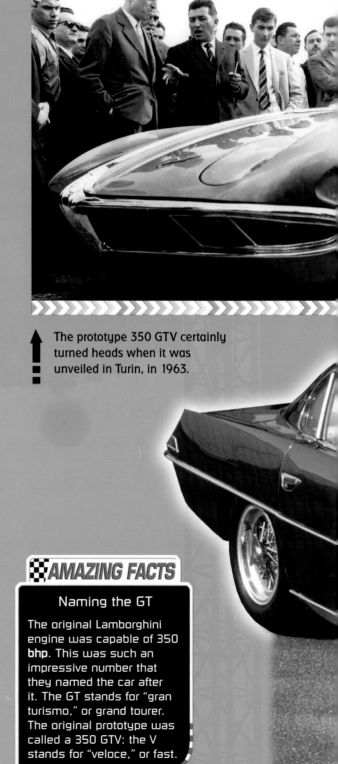

The prototype 350 GTV certainly turned heads when it was unveiled in Turin, in 1963.

🏁 AMAZING FACTS

Naming the GT

The original Lamborghini engine was capable of 350 **bhp**. This was such an impressive number that they named the car after it. The GT stands for "gran turismo," or grand tourer. The original prototype was called a 350 GTV: the V stands for "veloce," or fast.

12

Trial and error

But the car was not ready to run. Beneath the hood, a crate of ceramic tiles provided weight in place of an engine. Bizzarrini's engine, on display beside the car, was too large to fit under the hood. After Turin, chief engineer Dallara got to work modifying the engine, lowering its profile so it could fit in the car. Because Ferruccio thought the initial engine was "too high strung," Dallara also worked to control the power output, building a car more suited to a road than a racetrack.

■
■
|
↓
The 350 GTV looked beautiful—but there were still problems to be ironed out before a production model could be properly developed.

Keeping quiet

The troubleshooting didn't stop there. When the first transmissions, supplied by the German company ZF, produced too much noise, Dallara and his crew created their own design to quiet things down. Finally, when the company that had built the prototype body proved too small to mass-produce the 350 GTV, Lamborghini turned to Carrozzeria Touring to adjust the design and create the finished product.

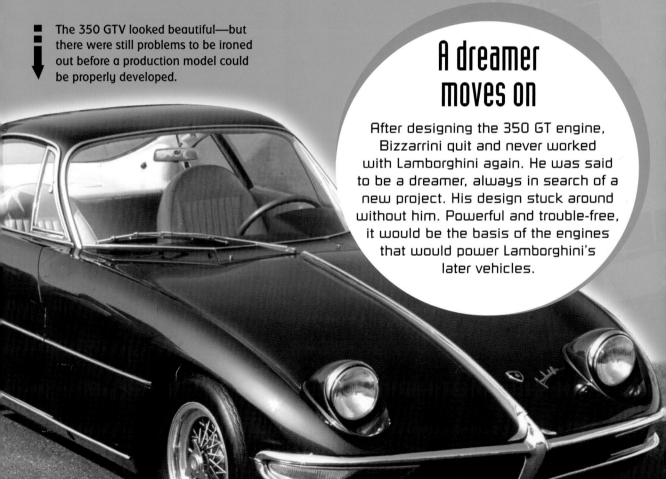

A dreamer moves on

After designing the 350 GT engine, Bizzarrini quit and never worked with Lamborghini again. He was said to be a dreamer, always in search of a new project. His design stuck around without him. Powerful and trouble-free, it would be the basis of the engines that would power Lamborghini's later vehicles.

The 350 GT

The new 350 GT debuted at the Geneva Show in March 1964, with a proper engine under its hood. Sound insulation was added, and the profile smoothed to make it more **aerodynamic**. Ferruccio was pleased enough with the response to move on to production. The first cars retailed at US$15,600—the equivalent of US$111,000 today.

For the 350 GT, the pop-up headlights were replaced with exposed ones, and the amount of ornamentation was reduced.

Vital Statistics

350 GT

Production years: 1964–66
No. built: 135
Top speed: 156 mph (251 km/h)
Engine type: 60-degree V12, front mounted, aluminum alloy
Engine size: 3464 cc (3.5 liter), 280 hp
Cylinders: 12
Transmission: 5-speed manual, rear-wheel drive
CO_2 emissions: N/A
EPA fuel economy ratings: N/A
Price: US$13,900

Critical acclaim

The V12 engine provided a lot of raw power, but the gearbox was smooth enough to let drivers easily slip into fifth gear at 60 mph (97 km/h). The weight of the vehicle was evenly distributed between the front and back wheels, improving how the car handled on the road. In spite of the low roofline, the car's interior was roomy and full of light. Testers could not make up their minds which was better—Lamborghini's 350 GT or Ferrari's 275 GTB, but most agreed that the Lamborghini was quieter.

Not all plain sailing...

The first Lamborghinis had problems, though. Many of those early cars were returned to the factory for repairs, which slowed production in the first few months. The company learned from its mistakes, though, and made improvements.

Car competition

The Lamborghini 350 GT came out alongside such supercars as the Aston Martin DB5 and the Corvette Sting Ray. Other competitors included the Jaguar E-Type and Maserati's Mistral 3700. Most comparisons are made with the Ferrari 275 GTB, however. "Motor Trend Classic" named the Ferrari 275 GTB the "Greatest Ferrari of all time," but Lamborghini's 350 GT matched up well to Ferrari's speed and elegance. It was also quieter.

The interior of the 350 GT, which reviewers called "a delight to drive."

400 GT and 400 GT 2+2

In 1965, Lamborghini offered a larger, four-liter engine for his 350 GT cars. The new class of vehicle produced was called the 400 GT. In 1966, the design of the 400 GT changed—raising the roofline and shrinking the rear window made room for two rear seats. This car became known as the 400 GT 2+2. It also featured a new, Lamborghini-produced five-speed gearbox to control a more powerful engine. With **torque** delivered to the wheels more efficiently, traction improved.

Vital Statistics

400 GT & 400 GT 2+2

Production years: 1966–67
No. built: 247
Top speed: 156 mph (251 km/h)
Engine type: Modified 350 GT, 60-degree V12
Engine size: 3929 cc (4 liter), 320 hp
Cylinders: 12
Transmission: 5-speed manual
CO_2 emissions: N/A
EPA fuel economy ratings: N/A
Price: US$10,000

The 400 GT proved more popular than the 350 GT, which ceased production in 1967. By 1968, 247 had been sold.

The 3500 GTZ

Worried about the financial stability of Carrozzeria Touring, Lamborghini sent two 350 GTs to the top coachmaker Zagato to test their abilities as bodymakers. Zagato produced two sporty vehicles with a higher roofline and a flatter front windshield. The 3500 GTZ debuted at the 1965 London Motor Show. A deal between Lamborghini and Zagato never materialized, and these were the only two 3500 GTZs ever built.

What next?

In two short years, Lamborghini had produced a vehicle that turned heads at a number of auto shows and had wowed critics. But more importantly, Lamborghini had matured as a car company, learning from its mistakes and modifying its designs to produce a popular and well-built vehicle. Ferruccio may have wanted to build a perfect car from the start, but when that proved impossible, he dedicated his company to work toward that perfection over time.

The 400 GT 2+2 had better road handling—and two extra seats, so passengers could also enjoy the ride.

Chapter 3

Lamborghini Rises »»»»

At the end of May 1966, Lamborghini development engineer Bob Wallace drove a new Lamborghini to a casino at the start of the Monaco Grand Prix. The car wasn't there to race, but even parked alongside some of the fastest cars in the world, the Lamborghini attracted a crowd. This car was the prototype of the Miura.

Birth of the Miura

With the GT line established and doing well, the Lamborghini engineering team wanted to build on its success. The Miura would confirm Lamborghini's place as a builder of supercars. But the drive to build the Miura came almost in spite of Ferruccio's own efforts. Dallara, Stanzani, and Wallace thought up the vehicle on their own, when one of the last things Ferruccio wanted to build was a racecar.

The first Miura—the prototype P400—was actually an idea that three of Ferruccio's engineers came up with.

Ferruccio racing

Ferruccio was soured to racing in 1948, when he entered the Fiat Topolino he had rebuilt and modified into the 1,000-mile Mille Miglia race. His short racing career came to a bad end when he drove the Fiat into the side of a restaurant near Turin!

Cars for the driver

As a result, Lamborghini's first cars were designed with the driver experience in mind—and not with the intent of winning races. Most Italian carmakers sought to dominate through speed, and Ferruccio wanted to concentrate on other aspects of the driver's experience. So the Lamborghini company would not test its cars on the Formula 1 circuit while Ferruccio owned Lamborghini.

Going it alone

But Ferruccio's stance frustrated his engineers, who were used to testing their engine design on the racetrack. As a result, Dallara, Stanzani, and Wallace started work on the P400 (the Miura prototype) in their spare time. When Ferruccio found out, he allowed the work to continue, seeing the potential for the vehicle. But he insisted the car would not be raced.

Bob Wallace

A racecar driver from New Zealand, Bob Wallace joined Lamborghini in 1963 as a mechanic. However, his driving skills and his ability to clearly explain any problems he experienced when he was driving test vehicles got him noticed. Wallace is best known for his work on the Miura. He was involved in its design, and he personally unveiled it to the public by driving it to the Monaco Grand Prix in May 1966.

Designing the Miura

The idea Dallara, Stanzani, and Wallace had of mounting the engine in the middle of the car, **transverse** (with the crankshaft side-to-side, relative to the car), was pretty radical. Only a handful of car builders had tried it. Mounting an engine as powerful as a Lamborghini V12 transverse was completely unheard of.

Bodywork

To save space, the engineers merged the transmission and the **differential** into the engine. The chassis for the automobile debuted at the 1965 Turin Salon. Impressed onlookers actually ordered the car—even though the body for the vehicle had not yet been designed. For this, Lamborghini turned to Carrozzeria Bertone.

Vital Statistics

Miura P400S

Production years: 1969–71
No. built: 140
Top speed: 172 mph (277 km/h)
Engine type: 60-degree V12, mid-mounted transverse
Engine size: 3929 cc (4 liter), 370 hp
Cylinders: 12
Transmission: 5-speed manual, rear-wheel drive
CO_2 emissions: N/A
EPA fuel economy ratings: 11 mpg
Price: US$16,750

Moving the engine toward the rear of the car allowed Lamborghini to lower the Miura's hood. The changes produced an even more aerodynamic design without sacrificing room in the cab.

A beautiful machine

Bertone's **coupe** featured smooth, balanced, aerodynamic curves that combined the sleek look of a racecar with the finished look of a luxurious street vehicle. Little details include the "eyelashes" (slatted grilles) around the pop-up headlights. Though the Miura sits low to the ground, large, wide-opening doors made it easy to get into and out of the car. All this combined for an impressive vehicle. The low profile of the car allowed it to handle corners with ease. Acceleration was smooth. The car could be hard to maneuver at slow speeds—but no one drove a Miura slowly!

The Jota

The Miura S Jota was a special car designed by Bob Wallace for GT racing. Wallace modified the suspension and the engine, reduced weight, and fitted larger rear wheels and a front spoiler. Wallace never got a chance to race it, as Ferruccio forbade it, and the car was sold to an enthusiast, after which it crashed into a bridge and was destroyed. Others have copied the Jota design, modifying production Miuras.

The Bob Wallace-designed special-edition Miura—the Jota. Only one was ever made.

⟩⟩ Increasing sales

When the Miura was introduced, there was no direct rival on the market, and it took time before competitors like Ferrari could catch up. As production started in late 1966, Lamborghini thought he would be lucky to sell 50 Miuras. Within three years, 474 had sold. Upgrades to the original model include the P400S and the P400SV, which increased the engine's pull to 385 hp and top speeds to 180 mph (290 km/h).

Lamborghini grows

The Miura entered production at just the right time for Lamborghini. The 350 GT impressed critics—but the Miura blew them away. Ferrari and Maserati had nothing like it on the market. By 1966, Lamborghini's sales were increasing and the company was expanding. Over 300 employees worked at the factory at Sant'Agata.

🏁 AMAZING FACTS

Sinatra's Miura

Among many celebrity Miura owners was Frank Sinatra. Legend has it that he traveled to the factory himself and asked for one to be built in his favorite color—orange. He had the interior of his Lamborghini Miura retrimmed in wild boar hide.

The P400SV was an upgrade to the two earlier Miura models— the P400 and the P400S.

The Islero

As successful as the Miura had been, Ferruccio knew he couldn't rest on his laurels. In 1968, Lamborghini introduced the Islero. Continuing Ferruccio's love of bullfighting, this car was named after a bull that killed a famous bullfighter named Manuel Rodriguez. The Islero was an updated 400 GT—a two-seater featuring a front-mounted, four-liter V12 engine capable of 320 bhp and a top speed of 159 mph (256 km/h).

▪ The Islero was four inches (ten cm) shorter than the 400 GT 2+2, and 400 pounds (183 kg) lighter. It had an all-steel body and retractable headlamps.

Islero GT & Islero GTS

Production years: 1968–70
No. built: 225 (both models)
Top speed: 159 mph (256 km/h)
Engine type: 60-degree V12, front-mounted, aluminum alloy
Engine size: 3929 cc (4 liter), 320 hp (Islero), 350 hp (Islero S)
Cylinders: 12
Transmission: 5-speed with **synchromesh**
CO_2 *emissions:* N/A
EPA fuel economy ratings: N/A
Price: N/A

The Marzal

The Marzal was a **concept car** unveiled at the Geneva Motor Show in 1967. This four-seater featured **gullwing** doors, and the cab was surrounded by windows—even on the body of the door. Although a unique car, the ideas explored by the Marzal came to be used in the Espada. The design was an instant hit with children and die-cast collectors, as both Dinky and Matchbox toymakers produced thousands of scale models of the car for many years.

23

Islero style

What made the Islero so different from the Miura or the 400 GT was its styling. The smooth, curved lines were replaced with a sharper, more conservative look. The straighter lines allowed the company to get rid of the expensive curved windows of the 350 GT model.

The Islero was intended to be the Lamborghini for the masses, but despite the designers' best efforts, it was not to be. It never became the great success Ferruccio had hoped for.

The forgotten Lamborghini

Carrozzeria Marazzi, the company brought on board to style the body, wasn't equipped to meet the high standards of Lamborghini in the time it had available. Drivers complained about sloppy finishing inside the car.

Lamborghini adjusted the design in 1969, producing the Islero S, featuring an improved suspension and a redesigned interior, but it was too late. Sales didn't take off, and the Islero has been called the "forgotten" or "unloved" Lamborghini.

When the Islero ceased production in 1970, only 225 had been sold—100 of those the Islero S.

The Espada

At the same time as Ferruccio unveiled the Islero, the company produced a full four-seater called the Espada, which debuted in 1968. The car featured a flamboyant body designed by Bertone.

Mechanically, the Espada was similar to the 400 GT, with the four-liter V12 engine capable of producing 325 bhp. The transmission was also the same as offered on the Islero, using Lamborghini's own gearbox and final-drive unit. All of this sat on a redesigned chassis, using square tubes to reduce weight while maintaining structural strength. The wheelbase was longer to provide space for four passengers inside the cab. The interior was bright, thanks to large front and back windscreens.

Vital Statistics

Espada

Production years: 1968–78
No. built: 1,217
Top speed: 158 mph (254 km/h)
Engine type: 60-degree V12, front-mounted, aluminum alloy
Engine size: 3929 cc (4 liter), 325 bhp
Cylinders: 12
Transmission: 5-speed manual, rear-wheel drive, with synchromesh
CO_2 emissions: N/A
EPA fuel economy ratings: N/A
Price: US$16,800

The Espada was low to the ground and featured a long, low front hood. The local press believed it was a special motor show product, not a "family" car.

▶▶ Praise and failure

Despite its bulky appearance—it was almost six feet (1.8 m) wide—the Espada matched the performance and speed of other Lamborghinis. Reviewers praised the handling and the stability of the Espada, but it still wasn't perfect. Drivers complained that the instrumentation was confusing and hard for them to see, and the interior finish was criticized.

Updated versions of the Espada added a more powerful 350 bhp engine, a lowered floor to increase headroom, and a neater interior.

▶▶▶▶▶▶▶▶▶▶▶▶▶▶▶▶▶▶▶▶▶

The refinement of the Espada's V12 engine, plus the addition of sound-proofing, kept noise inside the car to a minimum.

New decade—new car

In 1970, Ferruccio launched the Jarama 2+2—a new model to replace the Islero. This would be the last front-engined Lamborghini sports car. It ditched the tubular chassis of the Islero and used a shortened version of the Espada. Bertone was again asked to design the body and came up with a sleek, low-profiled car, with flared wheel arches, curved side windows, and partially shielded headlamps.

Lacking the wow factor

The front-mounted engine had a simpler switchgear than previous models. Early Jaramas were capable of 350 bhp, while the Jarama S, introduced in 1972, could boast a Miura-like 365 bhp. The interior of the car was again fitted with high-quality leather, although the work-manship was variable. Despite the improvements, the Jarama sold only a little better than the unloved Islero it was designed to replace. By the time production ceased in 1978, only 327 of these cars had been produced.

Vital Statistics

Jarama

Production years: 1970–78
No. built: 177 (Jarama), 150 (Jarama S)
Top speed: 162 mph (261 km/h)
Engine type: 60-degree V12, front-mounted, aluminum alloy
Engine size: 3929 cc (4 liter), 350 bhp
Cylinders: 12
Transmission: 5-speed manual, rear-wheel drive with synchromesh
CO_2 emissions: N/A
EPA fuel economy ratings: N/A
Price: US$13,815

Made for drivers?

The geography of Italy may be why the country boasts so many sports-car companies. High mountain roads twist and turn, yet speed limits range from 55 to 60 mph (90 to 110 km/h) on rural roads and 80 mph (130 km/h) on highways. Today, these speeds are rigorously enforced by photo radar, but in the 1960s it was easier to go faster! Many companies tested their vehicles on roads between Modena and Rome.

The shielded headlights and a curved nose gave the Jarama a distinctive front "face."

Chapter 4
Lamborghini After Ferruccio »»»

By 1970, Automobili Lamborghini—though only seven years old—was one of the giants of fine Italian automakers. But the world was growing more difficult for the makers of high-powered automobiles. In the 1960s, a group of oil-producing countries in north Africa and the Middle East joined together to form OPEC (the Organization of the Petroleum Exporting Countries), to increase the **revenues** they received from the **export** of oil.

OPEC effects

The formation of this organization increased the price of oil and gasoline throughout Europe and North America. For the Western world, which had relied on cheap oil to fuel the economic boom of 1950s and 1960s, driving suddenly became a lot more expensive. The cost of goods went up, factories shut down, and people lost jobs. By 1973, the oil-producing nations of the Middle East began an oil **embargo** against Western nations (particularly the United States). The price of oil quadrupled, and stock markets crashed.

No more cheap oil

OPEC includes Algeria, Angola, Ecuador, Iran, Iraq, Kuwait, Libya, Nigeria, Qatar, Saudi Arabia, the UAE, and Venezuela. In 1973, it controlled 52 percent of the oil market. It became less powerful when more oil was discovered in parts of North America and as western economies became more fuel-efficient. Still, OPEC nations hold two-thirds of the world's oil reserves and one-third of the world's production.

Looking to the future

The oil crisis hammered home to Ferruccio something he had been thinking about for over three years—with oil becoming more expensive, and Europe's economy weakening, it was no longer profitable to build high-performance automobiles.

Already, there were laws demanding that vehicles use less fuel, and such laws were blocking Ferruccio's efforts to sell his cars to America. The future, it seemed, belonged to smaller, slower, more fuel-efficient vehicles.

Handing over the reigns

In 1973, Ferruccio Lamborghini contacted Georges-Henri Rossetti, a wealthy Swiss businessman and a friend, and sold him 51 percent of his stake in Automobili Lamborghini for US$600,000. Ferruccio continued to work at the Sant'Agata factory, hoping the situation would improve. It didn't. In 1974, he sold his remaining 49 percent stake to René Leimer, a friend of Rossetti. This was the beginning of a long period of instability.

By 1974, Ferruccio had sold Lamborghini. He saw no future for high-powered luxury automobiles. If its founder had given up, what hope was there for the company?

Continuing the work

Leimer and Rossetti were successful businessmen, but neither had run an automobile company before. After Ferruccio left Lamborghini in 1974, the factory managers and engineers continued to work on cars that Ferruccio had begun. These included the Urraco and the Countach.

Is smaller better?

The Urraco was Ferruccio's attempt to produce a lighter, smaller car to rival the Ferrari Dino and the Porsche 911. Although a four-seater, this small, slick sports car boasted a 2.5-liter engine that departed from the Lamborghini standard by using eight cylinders instead of 12. Like the Miura, the engine was mounted near the rear of the car, allowing the company to maintain a low profile in front.

Vital Statistics

Urraco P200/P250

Production years: 1972–79
No. built: 77 (P200), 520 (P250)
Top speed: 143 mph (230 km/h)
Engine type: 90-degree V8, mid-mounted, aluminum alloy
Engine size: 2463 cc (1994 cc, P200), 220 bhp
Cylinders: 8
Transmission: 5-speed manual, rear-wheel drive, with synchromesh
CO_2 emissions: N/A
EPA fuel economy ratings: 18 mpg
Price: US$14,500

■■➡

Once in production, the Urraco was praised for its strong and trouble-free performance. Bertone's coupe body was liked for its sleek lines and thin, aerodynamic design.

The Urraco family

Problems with the engine delayed production until after Lamborghini was sold. Complicating development was new antipollution legislation that required the Urraco's engines to be more efficient. Eventually, three models were produced: the P200, which featured a two-liter engine, the P250, which featured 2.5 liters, and the improved P300, unveiled later, which offered a three-liter engine and an improved transmission but which was more expensive. In these cars, Lamborghini took care to improve the interiors to address the concerns raised by drivers.

 High-quality leather trim was used in the Urraco, and the confusing central console eliminated, with the dashboard redesigned so that all dials and instruments were clearly seen by the driver.

Urraco Bravo

In 1974, Bertone put an experimental body on an Urraco P300 and showed it off at the Turin Auto Show. Rectangular slats covering the rear window were matched by similar slats covering the hood. The windows were tinted almost black. The car could run; it was a serious prototype for a possible replacement for the Urraco. The Urraco Bravo drove more than 40,000 miles (65,000 km) before it was retired.

The Silhouette

Hoping to expand its line, Lamborghini adapted the Urraco model and developed the Silhouette. Bertone designed a sleek racing body, with clean, straight lines and a wedge-shape that promised speed. The two-seater boasted a V8 engine designed to compete with Ferrari's 308 GTB. The model debuted at the 1976 Geneva Motor Show.

Success and failure

In spite of the production delays, the Urraco sold steadily throughout the second half of the 1970s, with 787 produced by the time the line was retired in 1979. The Silhouette wasn't so successful. The company couldn't get U.S. certification of the car and so only 52 were built before production ceased in 1978.

Vital Statistics

Silhouette P300

Production years: 1976–79
No. built: 54
Top speed: 160 mph (260 km/h)
Engine type: 90-degree V8, mid-mounted, aluminum alloy
Engine size: 2995 cc (3 liter), 260 bhp
Cylinders: 8
Transmission: 5-speed manual, rear-wheel drive, with synchromesh
CO_2 *emissions:* N/A
EPA fuel economy ratings: N/A
Price: Unknown

The move to a smaller car with the Silhouette had not proved as profitable as the company hoped, and it was four years before Lamborghini tried again.

The Countach

If Lamborghini's attempt to go small hadn't worked well, the company's efforts at the high end would bolster its reputation as a builder of premium high-performance automobiles. The Countach was commissioned by Ferruccio in 1970 to replace the famed Miura. Working with Bertone, Ferruccio unveiled the prototype at the 1971 Geneva Motor Show.

Ferruccio's parting gift

Painted bright yellow and featuring doors that opened up like the blades of scissors, the Countach had a mid-mounted engine, abandoning the Miura's transverse design that other carmakers were only just catching up to. Leading the development of the Countach, Giampaolo Stanzani—now Lamborghini's chief engineer—was clear on what the car was to be: a *macchini sportive stradalei*, a stable car on the road but easy to maneuver, offering comfort and luxury to both driver and passenger.

Mounting the Countach engine further forward shifted the weight of the car forward, improving how it handled at high speeds.

Lamborghini gas guzzlers

Thanks to the oil crisis, the average fuel economy of new cars rose from 17 miles (27 km) per gallon in 1978 to 22 miles (35 km) per gallon in 1982. Lamborghini lagged behind. The 1986 Countach could only travel six miles (ten km) per gallon in the city, and ten miles (16 km) on the highway.

Power and control

The Countach's production engine was the classic Lamborghini four-liter V12, capable of producing 375 bhp. Stanzani also designed a new chassis, using round metal tubes in order to reduce weight without sacrificing strength. The structure included a **roll cage** to protect the driver and passengers in case of an accident—a necessity since the prototypes were topping out at speeds of over 167 mph (270 km/h)!

Praise for the Countach

Mark Hughes, driving the twentieth production Countach, wrote a review praising the vehicle for *Classic & Sports Car* magazine: "With the mass so low and centered, handling is unimpeachable…. A twisty road reveals uncannily faithful responses to steering and throttle. Driven with precision, the Countach does all— and more—you could wish of it, simply heading where it's directed." In fact, there was no shortage of praise, and 150 of these cars would be produced in the first five years, selling for US$27,500 each (approximately US$150,000 today).

Vital Statistics

Countach LP400

Production years: 1974–78
No. built: 150
Top speed: 192 mph (308 km/h)
Engine type: 60-degree V12, mid-mounted, aluminum alloy
Engine size: 3929 cc (4 liter), 375 bhp
Cylinders: 12
Transmission: 5-speed manual, rear-wheel drive, with synchromesh
CO_2 emissions: N/A
EPA fuel economy ratings: N/A
Price: US$27,500

The Countach replaced the Miura as Lamborghini's show car. It could credibly claim to be the fastest *production car* in the world.

AMAZING FACTS

Countach

"Countach" is an exclamation Piedmont men say upon seeing a beautiful woman. Legend has it that automobile stylist Nuccio Bertone cried out "countach!" when he saw the prototype. Until then, the car had been referred to as "Project 112."

The interior of the Countach LP400—a car designed for owners for whom money was no object!

Decline, takeover, and rise

In spite of Rossetti's and Leimer's efforts to keep Lamborghini afloat, the company's financial troubles increased. Finally, in 1978, the owners had no choice but to declare **bankruptcy** and let the Italian courts take over. Lamborghini operated under caretakers for two years, until it was handed over to two Swiss brothers, Jean-Claude and Patrick Mimran.

A fresh start

Jean-Claude and Patrick had made their fortune as food entrepreneurs, and both had a passion for sports cars. They jumped at the chance to own the famed automaker. The brothers led the company out of **receivership** in 1984, injecting millions of dollars into the carmaker, upgrading the factory at Sant'Agata, and hiring new engineers and design talent from around the world.

The Quattrovalvole

The efforts of the Mimran brothers led to the unveiling of a modified Countach, called the Quattrovalvole. It offered an engine with fuel injection through four valves in each cylinder. This system pumped fuel into the engine faster and, coupled with the larger 5.2-liter engine, meant power—455 horsepower. Top speed increased to 178 mph (286 km/h), and the Quattrovalvole could go from 0 to 60 mph (97 km/h) in 5.1 seconds.

In 1984, Lamborghini finally succeeded in getting the Countach certified for the American market, making it easier for U.S. customers to purchase. A new and big market was opening up for the company.

The Countach was the most successful Lamborghini up to the 1980s, and the company continued turning it out for over 15 years. By the time production ceased in 1990, 1,326 Countachs had been made.

The Jalpa

In 1982, Giulio Alfieri, one of the new engineers recruited by the Mimran brothers, introduced the Jalpa. It was a revival of the Silhouette, using a larger (3.5-liter) V8 engine, able to produce 255 hp. The Jalpa smoothed out the Silhouette's rough edges. Greater care was also taken to improve the quality and layout of the interior.

AMAZING FACTS

The Jalpa look

Reflecting 1980s' fashions of big hair and shoulder pads, the Jalpa offered an optional, very large rear aerofoil, which served only for the look. Enthusiasts today recommend that those buying such a Jalpa discard it as soon as possible!

Vital Statistics

Jalpa P350

Production years: 1982–88
No. built: 421
Top speed: 150 mph (241 km/h)
Engine type: 90-degree V8,
  mid-mounted, aluminum alloy
Engine size: 3485 cc (3.5 liter),
  250 bhp
Cylinders: 8
Transmission: 5-speed manual
  rear-wheel drive, with synchromesh
CO_2 *emissions:* N/A
EPA fuel economy ratings: N/A
Price: US$40,750

Ferruccio after Lamborghini

After selling his car company, Ferruccio worked on his heating and cooling business. In 1980, he set up Lamborghini Oleodinamica, building hydraulic valves. After that, he retired to a 750-acre estate in Umbria, Italy, produced wines, and designed his own golf course. In 1993, he died of a heart attack at the age of 76.

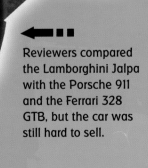

Reviewers compared the Lamborghini Jalpa with the Porsche 911 and the Ferrari 328 GTB, but the car was still hard to sell.

37

Chapter 5

Chrysler Joins In ≫≫≫≫

By the late 1980s, the Mimran brothers had had enough. Lee Iacocca of Chrysler came forward, buying Lamborghini outright in April 1987, for US$25.2 million. Iacocca was already famous for saving Chrysler from bankruptcy. Lamborghini's board of directors thought that if anybody could save their company, it was Lee Iacocca.

A new lease on life?

Chrysler gave Lamborghini a new lease on life, but it also gave the company no end of headaches. The cultures of the two companies were very different, and they could not see eye to eye on many projects. Still, the Chrysler years included the creation of one of Lamborghini's best-known and best-loved cars.

After buying Lamborghini, Iacocca spent another US$50 million, paying off debts and upgrading equipment. He set about recruiting engineers and designers from outside the company to shake things up. One such recruit was Luigi Marmaroli, who was to play a large part in what came next.

■■➤

Lee Iacocca was interested in competing with Ferrari in the "extra premium sports car" market and thought the reputation and talent behind Lamborghini would put him on the fast track.

Saving Chrysler

When Iacocca was hired by Chrysler, the company was nearly bankrupt, losing $1.2 billion in 1979 due to recalls of poorly designed vehicles. Iacocca secured a $1.5 billion loan guarantee from the U.S. government. He then set to work rebuilding the company, selling off unprofitable divisions, and introducing successful new vehicles. By 1983, Chrysler was profitable again, and the loans had been paid off ahead of schedule.

Diablo!

Marmaroli arrived from Alfa Romeo in 1985 and signed on to be Lamborghini's chief engineer. He set to work on a new project called the P132—soon to be called the Diablo. The company shopped around for designers and settled on Marcello Gandini, the designer of the Miura and the Countach, who had left Bertone to work freelance.

Early modifications

After the prototype failed to produce the increase in speed Lamborghini had hoped for, Chrysler helped redevelop the engine. It now offered a 5.7-liter capacity and an electronic fuel-injection system, promising an astounding 492 hp.

The Diablo boasted an estimated top speed of 202 mph (325 km/h), making it the world's fastest production car.

Sleek quality

For the body of the Diablo, Gandini produced a design that was more aerodynamic than the Countach, with graceful, smooth lines offering a far neater look. A light metal alloy was used on the doors, while the engine cover, bumpers, and hood were built using a material of carbon fiber and fiberglass.

Interior luxury

The interior of the Diablo featured upholstery of high-quality leather, an adjustable steering wheel, and a better-designed instrument layout. The windows opened electrically, and a high-class sound system was offered. The new exhaust system and catalytic converter took up what used to be the luggage space in the back.

Vital Statistics

Diablo/Diablo VT

Production years: 1990–98
No. built: 2,655 (including variants)
Top speed: 325 km/h (202 mph)
Engine type: 60-degree V12, mid-mounted, all-alloy
Engine size: 5729 cc (5.7 liter), 492 bhp
Cylinders: 12
Transmission: 5-speed manual, rear-wheel drive, with synchromesh
CO_2 emissions: N/A
EPA fuel economy ratings: N/A
Price: US$246,750

Aerodynamic spoilers in front and back of the Diablo blended into the body of the car.

The Diablo VT

The Diablo debuted in 1990 to positive reviews and steady sales, but Lamborghini was not going to stop there. In 1993, the company unveiled the Diablo VT. Standing for "viscous traction," the VT offered four-wheel drive for additional power between the wheels and the road, making it a safer and easier car for drivers to manage at high speeds.

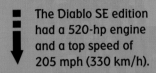
The Diablo SE edition had a 520-hp engine and a top speed of 205 mph (330 km/h).

Optional extras

Lamborghini also started offering optional extras for its Diablo. To celebrate the thirtieth anniversary of the company, the Diablo SE was introduced. The SE Jota was a limited-edition variant that claimed to have a 600-hp engine. In the years that followed, there were other limited-edition variants, including the **Roadster**, the SV, the SV Roadster, the GT, and the GTR. All used the same Diablo engine.

The anniversary Countach

Lamborghini hoped to unveil the Diablo in time for the company's twenty-fifth anniversary in 1988. When it was clear the car would not be ready at the time, a final version of the Countach was commissioned instead. The anniversary Countach was praised as the finest version of the car to be built.

41

The Rambo Lambo

As part of Lamborghini's drive to find new sources of revenue anywhere it could, work began on off-road military vehicles in 1977. The project hit snags over copyright claims, and progress was slow, but the engineers kept working until, in 1986, the four-wheel drive LM 002 debuted. LM stands for "Lamborghini Militaria"—Military Lamborghini—but the vehicle was popularly known as the Rambo Lambo. The Rambo was unsuited for the road, and the military decided it was too complex.

Vital Statistics

LM 002

Production years: 1986–92
No. built: 301 (plus 2 prototypes)
Top speed: 209 km/h (130 mph)
Engine type: 60-degree V12, front-mounted, light alloy
Engine size: 5167 cc (5 liter, 7 liter optional), 450 bhp
Cylinders: 12
Transmission: 4-wheel drive, ZF 5-speed gearbox with synchromesh
CO_2 emissions: N/A
EPA fuel economy ratings: N/A
Price: Unknown

Most Rambo Lambos were soon sold off to wealthy private owners. Nevertheless, over 300 were produced between 1986 and 1990.

The Genesis

In 1988, building on the concept of the Rambo Lambo LM 002, Lamborghini and Bertone produced a concept multipurpose vehicle (MPV) called the Genesis. This large vehicle had sliding rear doors, front doors opening in the Lamborghini gullwing fashion, and three rows of seats. It never went beyond the concept stage, and only one prototype was built.

Tension mounts

Despite the success of the Diablo, tensions built between Chrysler and Lamborghini. Executives disagreed on the direction of the company, starting with the move to hire Mauro Forghieri from Ferrari as technical director. Under Forghieri's influence, Lamborghini designed a V12 engine and chassis for a Formula 1 car. The engineers at Lamborghini were unsure about the wisdom of this move—they had acquired Ferruccio's distaste for racing—but Chrysler insisted.

Formula 1

By 1988, Lamborghini was ready to test its first in-house Formula 1 engine. Lamborghini claimed that the 3.5-liter V12 engine could produce over 600 hp. The company negotiated with F1 teams but got nowhere. Top teams shunned the newcomer. The smaller teams—with limited funding—did not have a chassis suitable for the Lamborghini engine. This poor response and bad luck soured Chrysler on the enterprise, and the Formula 1 project was shut down.

Lamborghini supplied engines to a number of F1 teams in 1989 and 1990, but the project was not a success.

The P140

There were also problems with a project to design a smaller-capacity car, code-named P140, that might have been called the Bravo. Gandini designed a body and Lamborghini went so far as to sign contracts with other companies to build the chassis. But Chrysler had not approved of this move. Hearing about it, Chrysler canceled the order, costing Lamborghini US$30 million.

Lamborghini after Chrysler

Lamborghini's return to profitability was brief. In 1992, sales crashed and Chrysler decided to sell the company, eventually turning it over to MegaTech in 1994. MegaTech was owned by an Indonesian company headed by Setiawan Djody and Tommy Suharto. Djody hired Michael Kimberly as Lamborghini's president and managing director.

Promoting Lamborghini

Kimberly studied Lamborghini's operations and decided that the company could not survive by making just one or two models. He also felt that the price of Lamborghinis needed to drop so that American car enthusiasts could afford them. Before he moved on these plans, however, he launched a marketing campaign to sell the heritage and mystique of the Lamborghini. By 1995, the campaign had helped to raise sales by 14 percent in the United States and 34 percent worldwide.

■ The new team at Lamborghini worked hard to promote models such as the Diablo in overseas markets, especially the U.S.A.

Cost-cutting

Although Kimberly improved sales, Lamborghini still lost money. The Indonesian managers hired Vittorio DiCapua in November 1996 to turn the company around. DiCapua slashed staff and cut costs in half. In 1996, Lamborghini needed to sell 450 Diablos to break even. DiCapua's measures moved that break-even point to 196 cars in 1997. That year, 209 Diablos were sold.

A new crisis

Though Lamborghini was in better shape, events around the world complicated things once more. An economic shock called "the Asian Crisis" hit Indonesia, causing Lamborghini's owners to look for buyers. A German company—Volkswagen AG—stepped forward, offering US$110 million. The ownership of Lamborghini was going back to Europe.

Based on the Diablo VT chassis, the Raptor was a one-off concept car shown in 1996.

The Raptor

The Raptor was a one-off concept car that combined the mechanics of a late-model Diablo with a body that had been designed by Zagato. The Raptor made its debut at the 1996 Geneva Salon. It was intended as the first in a limited-edition series, but a deal between Lamborghini and Zagato fell through. When Audi took over Lamborghini, the project was abandoned.

Chapter 6
≫Stability, Growth, Acclaim ≫ ≫ ≫ ≫

Thanks to restructuring, Lamborghini emerged near the twenty-fifth anniversary of Ferruccio's sale as a profitable, efficient company. Despite the years of uncertainty, the company had managed to produce two vehicles that wowed the public—the Countach and the Diablo. But just as Lamborghini was back in the black, it was sold off again, to Volkswagen of Germany.

New bosses—again

Lamborghini was intended to bolster the work of VW's luxury-car division, Audi. Lamborghini's managers and workers were nervous at first. Under Indonesian management money for development had been erratic, but there were fears that the German company's reputation for strict control would run counter to the Italian plant's self-disciplined culture and that Lamborghini's cars would lose their **flamboyant** character. Fortunately, these fears proved groundless.

■■➡

VW had plans to build on Lamborghini's reputation as a producer of some of the fastest production cars in the world.

Lamborghini's VW brothers

Volkswagen now owns three high-profile luxury performance-car companies: Britain's Bentley, France's Bugatti, and Italy's Lamborghini. All of these companies struggled before VW bought them out. Bentley and Lamborghini in particular have prospered, selling more vehicles and building their reputations since the takeover.

▪
▼ Audi believed that if the company's cars turned heads, their headquarters should do so, too, and invested money in expanding and improving the plant in Sant'Agata.

Bigger is better

Werner Mischke, the new chairman of Lamborghini, thought the company had to grow to survive. "We have to build up the business," he said in 2003. "Maybe in seven to ten years, we can be selling three thousand cars a year. We need to sustain volumes and that means **derivatives**. We need open versions as well as coupes. We have to discuss a third model."

Audi poured money into upgrading Lamborghini's facilities. The factory that Ferruccio built had hardly been changed since the 1960s. Audi bought more land around the factory, added buildings, and replaced the brick and concrete exterior with a modern glass façade.

Farewell to the Diablo

In car design, Audi had plans to replace the Diablo, but these couldn't be developed fast enough. While customers waited, Audi upgraded the Diablo, producing the Diablo 6.0 Liter. This could produce 550 hp, making it the most powerful production Lamborghini yet. Four-wheel drive came as standard, and the new Diablo shattered previous Lamborghini records. The top speed was estimated at 205 mph (330 km/h) and its **acceleration** from 0 to 100 mph (97 km/h) was a super-fast 3.4 seconds.

The new Diablo was only available for two years. In that time, a respectable 383 were produced. But this was only a taste of what was to come.

Vital Statistics

Diablo 6.0 Liter

Production years: 2000–01
No. built: 383 (including 45 SEs)
Top speed: 205 mph (330 km/h)
Engine type: 60-degree V12, mid-mounted, all alloy
Engine size: 5992 cc (6 liter), 500 bhp
Cylinders: 12
Transmission: VT 4-wheel drive as standard
CO_2 emissions: N/A
EPA fuel economy ratings: N/A
Price: US$239,000

What next?

The Diablo had helped maintain Lamborghini's reputation through its turbulent years under the leadership of Chrysler and MegaTech. While upgrades to the model had kept it fresh, they couldn't alter the fact that the design was now almost a decade old. Lamborghini's Audi managers knew that the task of replacing the Diablo would be their first big test.

The Murciélago

Audi recruited a Peruvian-born designer named Belgian Luc Donckerwolke to be Lamborghini's head of design. He set to work producing a four-wheel drive, mid-engine sports car with a low-slung coupe body. The engine that powered this vehicle—to be called the Murciélago—was one of Lamborghini's most powerful: a 6.2-liter V12, boasting 580 hp that could push the car from 0 to 60 mph (97 km/h) in 3.6 seconds.

■ The Murciélago was just over three feet
▮ (one m) high, and featured Lamborghini's
▼ classic scissor-action doors, as well as
   carbon-fiber and steel on the bodywork.

Luc Donckerwolke

Born in Lima, Peru, in 1965, Belgian Luc Donckerwolke joined Audi's design department in 1992, becoming Lamborghini's styling coordinator in 1998. He managed Lamborghini's design studio, which made him responsible for both the Murciélago and the Gallardo. Donckerwolke left Lamborghini in 2006 to work with the Spanish auto company SEAT.

>> Audi's attention to detail

Just as the Diablo updated the design of the Countach, the body of the Murciélago was an upgrade of the Diablo. The interior was greatly improved, too. The quality of the trim and the layout of the instruments made the car a driver's dream even before the engine started.

The bull that founded two dynasties

The Lamborghini Murciélago is named after a bull that survived 28 sword strikes during a legendary battle with famed bullfighter Rafael "El Lagartijo" Molina Sanchez in 1879. The bull was eventually given as a gift to Don Antonio Miura, who used it to father his breed of famed fighting bulls.

Murciélago

Production years: 2001–
No. built: over 4,000
Top speed: 205 mph (330 km/h);
  213 mph (342 km/h) in the LP 670-4
Engine type: 60-degree V12,
  mid-mounted, aluminum alloy
Engine size: 6192 cc, 6496 cc
  in LP versions, 580–661 bhp
Cylinders: 12
Transmission: 6-speed
CO_2 *emissions:* 500 g/km
EPA fuel economy ratings: 8 mpg
  (city); 13 mpg (highway)
Price: US$262,175

A rear spoiler and air scoops were integrated into the Murciélago, folding out at high speeds to help its aerodynamics and cool down the engine.

DC·145XN

Murciélago variations

At the 2003 Frankfurt Motor Show, Lamborghini unveiled the Murciélago R-GT, a model to be sold to individuals who wanted to race. It cut the weight of the vehicle from two tons (1,800 kg) to 1.2 tons (1,100 kg), and added wings and spoilers. In 2004, Lamborghini added a "roadster" version of the Murciélago (called Spyder), which came with a sign on the windshield that warned the drivers not to go more than 100 mph (160 km/h) with the cloth top in place in case it came off.

LP Murciélagos

Then, in 2005, Lamborghini upgraded the Murciélago with a series of "LP" models. Expanding the engine from 6.2 liters to 6.5, total horsepower rose from 572 to 631. Tuning this engine produced even more powerful models in the LP650-4, until finally the Murciélago LP670-4 SuperVeloce upgraded the engine's output to 661 hp.

The LP670-4—likely to be the last before the line is retired in 2012—boasts a top speed of 212 mph (342 km/h) and an acceleration from 0 to 100 mph (97 km/h) in 2.8 seconds.

AMAZING FACTS

Murciélago milestone

Lamborghini unveiled its 4,000th Murciélago on February 12, 2010. This milestone vehicle had bright orange paintwork. The Murciélago was shipped to China for display at the Lamborghini showroom in Hangzhou.

The Gallardo

With the Murciélago building on the heritage of the Miura, the Countach and Diablo, Lamborghini now turned to the task of building an updated version of the Urraco. Named the Gallardo, this vehicle would prove to be the most successful Lamborghini model to date.

Gallardo

Production years: 2003–
No. built: Over 10,000
Top speed: 192–202 mph (309–325 km/h)
Engine type: 90-degree V10, mid-mounted, aluminum alloy
Engine size: 4961–5204 cc, 562 bhp
Cylinders: 10
Transmission: 6-speed, 4-wheel drive
CO_2 emissions: 325–330 g/km
EPA fuel economy ratings: 11 mpg (city); 16 mpg (highway)
Price: US$180,000+

Small but powerful

Although smaller than a Murciélago, the Gallardo was far from underpowered. A five-liter V10 engine was installed, producing 492 hp. This two-seater had a top speed of 192 mph (309 km/h) and could accelerate from 0 to 100 mph (97 km/h) in 4.1 seconds. The engine sat low to the ground, which helped improve handling.

The LP560-4 model Gallardo was launched in 2008 and was offered in six-speed **manual** or six-speed E-gear (semiautomatic).

Gallardo bodywork

For the body, Lamborghini approached designer Giorgetto Giugiaro at Italdesign. Working with Donckerwolke, he produced a design that recalled the majesty of the Murciélago. It did not share the higher-end car's scissor-action doors and had a squarer profile, but the Gallardo had the same aerodynamic shape, and the interior is similarly well made, with luxurious seats and a sensibly designed dashboard.

The Superleggera

A variant of the Gallardo ("Superleggera" means "superlight" in Italian), this car debuted at the 2007 Geneva Motor Show. Its body was designed by Carrozzeria Touring. Touring had recently restarted business. Design changes made the Superleggera 220 pounds (100 kg) lighter than the standard Gallardo model, thanks to the use of carbon fiber. In 2011, the Gallardo LP 570-4 was released.

AMAZING FACTS

Gallardo milestone

Lamborghini unveiled its 10,000th Gallardo on June 25, 2010. The sleek vehicle was painted in a color known as "Midas yellow." Like the milestone Murciélago, the Gallardo ended up in China, in the hands of a private owner.

The Superleggera's 5.2-liter V10 engine can power the car from 0 to 60 mph (97 km/h) in 3.4 seconds.

Priced to match

When the Gallardo was launched, Lamborghini made a bold statement. The first models were sold for US$180,000—US$20,000 more than the competing Ferrari 360, and US$27,750 more than Porsche's 911 Turbo S. In contrast to Ferruccio selling his first 350 GTs at a loss to keep his prices competitive with Ferrari, the Gallardo was priced higher, making a point about its quality. If you wanted to drive one, you had to pay more for it. If customers objected, they did not say so by keeping their money in their wallets. Within two years of launch, over 2,000 Gallardos had sold.

Special editions and Spyders

Lamborghini followed up the Gallardo with more variants, a limited (250 units) special edition, the "Spyder" roadster version, then the Superleggera. All these shared the basic Gallardo engine.

In 2008, Lamborghini upgraded that engine, producing a series of LP versions of the Gallardo, with a 5.2-liter V10 engine producing up to 562 hp and capable of top speeds of up to 202 mph (325 km/h).

The Gallardo Spyder was launched at the Los Angeles Auto Show in 2008.

AMAZING FACTS

Running-in

Before a Lamborghini engine goes into a car, an electric motor drives each V12 for six hours before the engine is started up to run on its own. It then runs at various speeds for up to two hours at a time, after which engineers measure the engine's power and torque.

Good days for Lamborghini

In 1996, the Lamborghini plant produced 211 cars and did 34 million euros worth of business. By 2004, that number had grown by almost eight times the number of vehicles (1,592) and almost seven times the revenue (243 million euros). The company employed 714 workers and boasted a 311,077 square foot (28,900 sq m) modern factory complex.

Ferruccio's dream

The marriage between Audi and Lamborghini gave driving enthusiasts the best of both worlds: Lamborghini's boisterous flare and speed was combined with Audi's precision and attention to detail. Ferruccio founded Lamborghini embarking on a quest to build a perfect car. Nearly 50 years later, the dream may have been realized.

Gallardo police vehicles are used during emergencies on the Salerno-Reggio Calabria highway and to deliver organs needed for immediate transplantation.

Lamborghini police cars

You won't find Lamborghinis serving most police departments, but two were donated by the company to the Italian police force in December 2004. A third Gallardo was donated to the Italian police in 2008. Two more Gallardos are on loan to the London Metropolitan Police and are used in publicity events.

Chapter 7
Driving Into the Future »»»»»

On January 6, 2006, to celebrate the fortieth anniversary of the Miura, a concept car styled like the classic Miura was presented at the American Museum of Television and Radio, as part of the Los Angeles Auto Show. However, Lamborghini president and CEO Stephan Winkelmann denied that the Miura was retuning to production. "The Miura was a celebration of our history, but Lamborghini is about the future. Retro design is not what we are here for."

The unveiling of the concept Miura gave rise to rumors that the car would be reintroduced to production.

Secret tests

With the Murciélago almost a decade old, Lamborghini is working on a design to replace it. In January 2010, "spy" photos appeared showing what was supposed to be a matte-black prototype being tested in Scandinavia. Rumors suggest that the new model, possibly named the Jota, will offer a direct-inject V12 engine producing up to 700 hp, using carbon-fiber and aluminum components. We know this for sure: it will be luxurious, it will be expensive, and it will be fast.

Lucky partnership

Lamborghini is now a profitable venture for Audi, producing more cars in the past ten years than it did in the 35 years beforehand. Audi is happy with Lamborghini's performance, and Lamborghini's reputation has been enhanced by Audi's influence. It is likely that Lamborghini and Audi will work together for a long time to come.

The future?

Future Lamborghinis will no doubt use lighter and stronger materials. The company quickly adopted carbon fiber on its automobiles when it became available. It also uses aluminum components and a material called alcantara instead of leather to help reduce the weight of the cars. In July 2010, the company announced that it had set up an Advanced Composites Research Center at its Sant'Agata factory. The center promises not only to find new ways to put experimental new materials to use but new and better ways to produce such material.

The Reventón

The Reventón was an extremely limited-edition Lamborghini that debuted at the 2007 Frankfurt Motor Show. Selling for US$1.25 million each and boasting a 6.5-liter V12 engine producing 640 hp, it is one of the most powerful and expensive production cars in the world. Using a modified Murciélago engine, the Reventón can accelerate from 0 to 100 mph (97 km/h) in 3.4 seconds and reach a top speed of 221 mph (356 km/h).

Only 21 Reventóns were produced, each individually numbered, and with one sent directly to the Lamborghini museum.

Power to the driver

Lamborghini has no plans at present for a **hybrid** vehicle or an electric model, but that may change as oil gets scarcer and more expensive. The company will likely add new technologies that enhance the driving experience.

But it's worth remembering what Ferruccio wanted in his perfect car when he founded Lamborghini. He aimed to create a car without faults, that placed the driver in complete control over a powerful engine. For almost 50 years, Lamborghini has striven toward that goal. As the company moves into the future, one can only see its engineers working toward putting more power at a driver's fingertips.

A concept car such as the Estoque demonstrates how Lamborghini is constantly looking in new directions.

The Lamborghini museum

The Lamborghini museum is attached to the main building at Sant'Agata. It occupies two floors and displays a wide selection of old models, engines, and photographs covering the history of the company. The star of the show is the original 350 GTV prototype. There is also the prototype of the LM 002 and a selection of the various models of the Diablo.

Lamborghini at the races

Although it never returned to the Formula 1 circuit after 1993, Lamborghini wasn't through with racing. In 1996, Lamborghini sponsored the Lamborghini Class Challenge, where professional and amateur racers alike raced Diablo SVRs in a series of competitions throughout Europe. Drivers paid US$350,000 for the privilege of racing for two years. At the end of that period, the drivers got to keep their Lamborghinis. This racing series continued until 1998.

GT racing

The Diablo, the Murciélago, and the Gallardo have all appeared in "GT" races, where modified production cars rather than new vehicles are in competition. In 2007, Lamborghini entered Gallardos in the FIA GT3 and the Japanese "Super GT" Championship. The rules stated that the car still had to closely resemble the standard Gallardo production model. The Japanese Gallardo had to be changed into a rear-wheel drive vehicle, and its engine could produce no more than 295 hp.

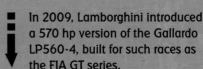

In 2009, Lamborghini introduced a 570 hp version of the Gallardo LP560-4, built for such races as the FIA GT series.

Lamborghini Timeline

1963	Lamborghini begins operations; the 350 GTV is unveiled at the Geneva Motor Show
1964	First 350 GT is delivered
1966	400 GT and Miura P400 are introduced
1968	Islero and Espada are introduced
1969	Miura P400S model is launched
1970	Jamara 2+2 is launched
1972	Urraco P250 and Jarama 400 GTS are introduced
1973	Oil embargo causes cost of oil to rise in the U.S.; Ferruccio sells 51 percent of Automobili Lamborghini to Georges-Henri Rossetti
1974	Ferruccio sells his remaining stake to René Leimer; Countach LP400 is produced
1976	Silhouette is introduced
1980	Mimram brothers buy the company and bring Lamborghini out of bankruptcy in 1984
1982	Countach LP500S and Jalpa are introduced
1984	Countach is certified for the U.S., opening up an important market for Lamborghini
1985	Designer Luigi Marmaroli joins Lamborghini
1986	Release of the off-road LM 002—the Rambo Lambo
1987	Mimran brothers sell Lamborghini to Chrysler
1988	Concept car Genesis is produced
1990	Final Countach is produced; Diablo and Diablo VT are introduced
1993	Ferruccio Lamborghini dies
1994	Chrysler sells Lamborghini to MegaTech
1996	President Vittorio Di Capua begins cost-cutting and restructuring program; one-off Raptor is unveiled
1998	Lamborghini is sold to VW's Audi division
2000	Final Diablo is launched
2001	Diablo is replaced by the Murciélago
2003	Gallardo is introduced; sales increase dramatically
2004	Roadster version of the Murciélago is released
2005	Start of the LP Murciélago models
2007	Gallardo Superleggera debuts at the Geneva Auto Show
2009	Lamborghini introduces a racing version of the Gallardo
2010	4,000th Murciélago is produced; 10,000th Gallardo is produced

Further Information

Books

Lamborghini
by Rebecca Hawley
(PowerKids, 2007)

Lamborghini: Forty Years
by David Joliffe with Tony Willard
(Motor Books International, 2004)

The Complete Book of Lamborghini
by Pete Lyons
(Publications International, 1988)

Lamborghini
by A. T. McKenna
(Abdo, 2002)

Lamborghini: Supercars from Sant'Agata
by Anthony Pritchard
(Haynes Publishing, 2005)

Web sites

www.lamborghini.com/
Official Lamborghini web site

www.lambocars.com/
Web site for enthusiasts, LamboCars

www.timpelen.com/
Web site for enthusiasts, Timpelen

www.automobilemag.com/features/news/0909_ferrari_vs_lamborghini_great_rival-ries/index.html
Automobile Mag: Great Rivalries: Ferrari vs. Lamborghini

elle-overdrive.blogspot.com/2008/05/lamborghini-and-ferraris-rivalry.html
Overdrive: Lamborghini and Ferrari's Rivalry

www.ehow.com/how_2095208_drive-lamborghini.html
How to drive a Lamborghini

Glossary

acceleration A measure of how quickly something speeds up

aerodynamic Describing something with a low amount of drag

alloy A substance consisting of two or more metals or of a metal and a nonmetal combined

automatic transmission A device that shifts a car's gears without help from the driver according to the speed the car is traveling

bankruptcy The reduction of a company or individual to a state of impoverishment

brake horsepower (bhp) The raw horsepower of an engine before the loss of power caused by the alternator, gearbox, differential, pumps, etc.

camshaft A rod in a car's engine; as the camshaft turns, it pushes the pistons up and down, compressing gas in the engine and powering the car

chassis The strong support structure that connects the engine to the wheels and holds the body to the car

concept car A vehicle made to show the public a new design or technology

coupe A hard-topped sports car with two seats

derivatives Different cars based on the same design

differential The function in a car that allows the wheels to move at different speeds

embargo A governmental law that does not allow trade with a specific country

export Something that is traded from one country to another

flamboyant Elaborate and showy

grand tourer A two-seat sports car that is made for driving long distances in comfort

greenfield An undeveloped area of land

gullwing Doors that open upward rather than out to allow the driver and passengers to enter

horsepower (hp) The amount of pulling power an engine has based on the number of horses it would take to pull the same load

hybrid A car that uses both a typical combustion engine and an electric system

manual transmission A device that a driver must operate to shift a car's gears

production car A car that is made in large numbers on an assembly line

prototype The original or test version of a car, which is later modified and developed into a production car

receivership The legal situation of a company that is reorganizing itself to try and avoid bankruptcy

revenues Income from sales of a product or service

Roadster A two-seater Lamborghini car with a soft-top roof and no rear or side windows; also known as a Spyder

roll cage A special frame built in the cab of a vehicle to protect the driver and passengers if the car overturns in an accident

synchromesh A system for shifting gears that allows them to revolve at the same speed, so that they can be shifted smoothly

torque A force that causes something to rotate or turn; in a car, the power that an engine generates by turning

transverse Lying across or crosswise

Index

Entries in **bold** indicate pictures

350 GT 11, 14, **14**, 15, **15**, 16, 22
350 GTV 11, 12, **12**, 13, **13**, 58
400 GT 16, **16**, 24, 25
400 GT 2+2 16, **17**
3500 GTZ 17

Alfa Romeo 5, 6, 9, 11, 39
Alfieri, Giulio 36
Audi 45, 46, 47, 48, 49, 55, 57
Automobili Lamborghini 5, 10, 28, 29

Bizzarrini, Giotto 10, 13
bullfighting 5, 23, 50

carbon fiber 40, 53, 56, 57
Carrozzeria Bertone 20, 21, 25, 27,
    31, 32, 33, 34, 39, 42
Carrozzeria Marazzi 24
Carrozzeria Touring 13, 17, 53
catalytic converters 40
chassis 11, 20, 25, 27, 34, 43, 44
Chrysler 38, 39, 43, 44, 49
Classic & Sports Car magazine 34
concept cars 23, 42, 45, 56, **56**, **58–59**
Corvette Sting Ray 15
Countach 30, 33, **33**, 34, **34–35**, **35**,
    36, **36**, 39, 40, 41, 46, 50, 52
    Countach LP400 34
    Countach Quattrovalvole 36

Dallara, Giampaolo 11, **11**, 13, 18, 19
Diablo 39, **39**, 40, **40**, 41, 42, 43, **44**,
    45, 46, 48, **48**, 49, 50, 58, 59
    Diablo 6.0-Liter 48
    Diablo GT 41
    Diablo GTR 41
    Diablo Roadster 41
    Diablo SE 41, **41**
    Diablo SV 41
    Diablo SV Roadster 41
    Diablo VT 40, 41
DiCapua, Vittorio 45
Djody, Setiawan 44
Donckerwolke, Belgian Luc 49, 53

engines 4, 7, 10, **10**, 11, 13, 14, 15,
    16, 20, 21, 23, 25, 26, **26**, 27, 30, 31,
    32, 33, 34, 36, 39, 41, 43, 49, 52, 54,
    56, 57, 58
Espada 11, 23, 26, **26**, 27

Ferrari, Enzo 8, 9, 10
Ferraris 5, 6, **8**, 10, 11, 15, 22, 30, 32,
    43, 54
Fiat 5, 11, 19
Forghieri, Mauro 43
Formula 1 11, 19, **43**, 43, 59
Frankfurt Motor Show 51, 57

Gallardo 49, 52, **52**, 53, 54, **54**, 55,
    59, **59**
    Gallardo Spyder 54, **54**
    Gallardo Superleggera 53, **53**, 54
Gandini, Marcello 39, 40, 44
Genesis 42
Geneva Motor Show 14, 23, 32, 33, 53
Giugiaro, Giorgetto 53
Grand Prix, Monaco 18, 19

Iacocca, Lee 38, **38**, 39
interiors 15, **15**, 24, 25, 26, 27, 31, **31**,
    36, 40, 50, 53
Islero 11, 23, **23**, 24, **24**, 25, 27

Jaguar E-Type 15
Jalpa 5, 36, 37, **37**
Jarama **26-27**, 27
Jota SE 41

Kimberley, Michael 44, 45

Lamborghini, Ferruccio 5, 6, 7, **6–7**,
    8, 9, **9**, 10, 11, 12, 13, 14, 17, 18, 19,
    21, 23, 25, 27, 28, 29, **29**, 30, 33, 37,
    43, 47, 54, 55, 58
Lamborghini Class Challenge 59
Lamborghini museum 58
Leimer, René 29, 30, 35
LM 002 (Rambo Lambo) 42, **42**, 58
logo 5, **5**
London Motor Show 17
Los Angeles Auto Show 56

Marmaroli, Luigi 38, 39
Marzal 23
Maseratis 5, 6, 9, 11, 22
MegaTech 44, 49
Mimran, Jean-Claude and Patrick
    35, 36, 38
Mischke, Werner 47
Miura 5, 11, 18, 19, 20, **20**, 21, 22, 23,
    24, 30, 33, 37, 52, 56

Miura P400 19
Miura P400S 20, 22
Miura P400SV 22, **22**
Miura S Jota 21, **21**
Miura, Don Eduardo 5, 50
Motor Trend Classic magazine 15
Murciélago 5, 49, **49**, 50, **50**, 51, **51**,
    52, 53, 56, 57, 59
    Murciélago LPs 51
    Murciélago R-GT 51
    Murciélago Spyder 51

oil crisis 28, 33
OPEC 28

P140 44
police cars 55, **55**
Porsches 11, 30, 54
prototypes 12, 13, 18, 19, 31, 34, 39,
    42, 56, 58

racing 19, 21, 43, 59
Raptor 45, **45**
Reventón 57, **57**
Rossetti, Georges-Henri 29, 30, 35

Sanchez, Rafael Molina 50
Sant'Agata plant 12, 22, 29, 35, 47,
    47, 55, 57, 58
Scaglione, Franco 11, 12
Silhouette 32, **32**, 36
Sinatra, Frank 22
Sporting Motorist magazine 6
Stanzani, Giampaolo 11, 18, 19, 33
Suharto, Tommy 44

tractors 4, 5, **6–7**, 8, 12
Turin Auto Show 12, 13, 31

Urraco 5, 30, **30–31**, 31, **31**, 32, 52
    Urraco Bravo 31
    Urraco P200 30, 31
    Urraco P250 30, 31
    Urraco P300 31

Volkswagen AG 45, 46, 47

Wallace, Bob 11, 18, 21
Winkelmann, Stephan 56

Zagato 16, 45